Easy-to-serve recipes for the

Pontoon Food

Jon and Erin Davis

Adventure Publications
Cambridge, Minnesota

Sherry : Paul,
HAPPY
Boating!
Nancy
2019

Dedication

We would like to dedicate this book to our family and friends, who provided inspiration and support.

Acknowledgments

We would like to acknowledge Brenna Slabaugh for being our food stylist; Carl, Candice and Curtis Andre for their help with recipe testing and helpful suggestions; as well as our family, who gave us advice and support along the way.

Cover and book design by Lora Westberg
Photos by Erin Davis
Edited by Emily Beaumont

Introduction

Cabins and lake homes are meant for friends and family! We gather around decks, patios and boats for lazy conversation and needed relaxation. Pontoon boats in particular are part of the lake magic, as you cruise around sharing food and beverages, and they've long been associated with the lake-living tradition.

These recipes have been collected with a few things in mind. First, we wanted to create basic, honest food with as few processed ingredients as possible. Next, the recipes needed to be easy to prepare because you want to spend time with your guests, not in the kitchen. Some do take a bit more effort than others, but many can be prepared a day in advance. Other recipes are conducive to using more adventurous ingredients for more interest. These are indicated with the label "for a creative touch."

We also wanted to have a wide selection of recipes that are dairy free, gluten free or vegetarian for those cooks needing to accommodate certain dietary restrictions. These recipes are indicated by the following abbreviations: df=dairy free, gf=gluten free, gfo=gluten free option and v=vegetarian.

We hope you enjoy this collection of recipes and tips—and that this book might contribute to many memories of entertaining at your favorite summer retreat!

Table of Contents

Caprese Salad Skewers

skewers

tips to make serving easy

We recommend using wooden skewers, as they are biodegradable and can even be used for campfire kindling.

For skewer recipes that are served cold, store prepared skewers in a large, flat, plastic container in a cooler until ready to eat.

For hot skewers, store them in a covered glass baking dish placed inside an insulated casserole carrier, or wrap the dish with a large bath towel to keep skewers warm until serving.

Where noted, skewers may be cut in half to make smaller portions. Use heavy kitchen shears to score the skewers in the middle first, and then you may snap them cleanly in two.

Each recipe in this chapter makes approximately 8-10 skewers.

Antipasto Skewers (gf) Makes 8-10 skewers

Italian for "before the meal," antipasto is traditionally a first course of cured meats and cheeses alongside pickled peppers and other vegetables. Here, classic Italian flavors are combined on a skewer for easy snacking.

Ingredients

8 ounces Monterey Jack cheese, cubed

6 ounces pepperoni slices

1 jar Italian-style mix of pickled vegetables,
   Giardiniera (cauliflower, carrots and peppers)

8-10 pepperoncini

1 pint cherry tomatoes

20 Kalamata olives, pitted

Note: Use high-quality pepperoni slices found in the deli section of your local grocery store (not the presliced frozen variety). If you cannot find high-quality pepperoni, you can substitute salami.

Directions

Alternate placing cheese, pepperoni slices (folded in quarters) and vegetables on skewers.

Bloody Mary Skewers (gf, v, df) Makes 8–10 skewers

These tasty snacks can be enjoyed alone or alongside Bloody Marys (page 76) for happy hour.

Ingredients

8 ounces small pickles, such as gherkins or cornichons

6 ounces green olives stuffed with pimentos (or your favorite stuffed green olives)

16 ounces pickled okra

12 ounces pickled green beans, cut into bite-sized pieces

1 bunch baby radishes, thickly sliced

Directions

Use short skewers (skewers cut in half). Alternate placing pickles and other vegetables on skewers. Serve with Bloody Marys (page 76).

Caprese Salad Skewers (gf, v) Makes 8–10 skewers

Thought to have originated on the island of Capri, off Italy's Amalfi Coast, Caprese salad is a refreshing and satisfying snack. The green, white and red of the basil, mozzarella and tomato resemble the Italian flag.

Ingredients

Salt and pepper to taste

16 ounces fresh mozzarella balls (bocconcini), halved

1 pint cherry tomatoes

Handful fresh basil leaves, quartered

Directions

Use short skewers (skewers cut in half). Lightly salt and pepper halved mozzarella balls. Alternate placing cherry tomato, mozzarella halves and basil on skewers.

Charcuterie Skewers (gf) Makes 8-10 skewers

High in protein and low in carbs, these skewers are great snacks for active days on the lake.

Ingredients

1 pound assorted meats, sliced, such as turkey and roast beef

1/2 pound assorted cheeses, cubed, such as Swiss and Gouda

For a creative touch:
Try salami, soppressata, capicola, manchego and Gruyère.

Directions

Use short skewers (skewers cut in half). Cut each slice of meat in half and fold into quarters. Alternate placing meats and cheeses on skewers.

Shrimp Cocktail Skewers (gf, df) Makes 8-10 skewers

Always a crowd-pleaser! You can make the cocktail sauce mild or spicy to your preference.

Ingredients

3/4 cup ketchup

2 tablespoons prepared horseradish

1 tablespoon Dijon mustard

3-5 drops Worcestershire sauce

1 pound shrimp, headless, shelled, deveined,
   fully cooked and cooled

Directions

In a large bowl, combine ketchup, horseradish, mustard and Worcestershire. Toss shrimp in cocktail sauce and coat evenly. Place shrimp on skewers. Serve cold.

Marinated Shrimp Skewers (gf, df) Makes 8-10 skewers

Here's a fun way to enjoy shrimp: cool and tangy, with an Italian flair!

Ingredients

1/4 cup extra-virgin olive oil

1/2 red bell pepper

1/2 celery stalk, coarsely chopped

16 Kalamata olives, pitted

1 clove garlic

1 1/2 tablespoons lemon juice (about half a lemon)

Handful fresh parsley

Salt and pepper

1 pound shrimp, precooked

Directions

Combine olive oil, bell pepper, celery, olives, garlic, lemon juice, parsley, salt and pepper in a food processor; blend until smooth. Add shrimp to marinade and let sit in fridge for at least 30 minutes or up to 2 hours. Place shrimp on skewers. Serve cold.

Note: Do not prepare this the day ahead, as the shrimp will continue to cook in the lemon juice and will become tough.

Chicken Satay Skewers (gfo, df) Makes 8–10 skewers; entrée serves 4–6

Satay is a wildly popular street food throughout Indonesia and Malaysia, where you can find numerous versions of grilled meat skewers, seasoned and served with a spicy sauce. Our version incorporates a typical variation—spicy peanut sauce—into a marinade that bakes right into the chicken. These are almost as tasty served cold as leftovers as they are right out of the oven.

Note: As an alternative to baking, grill skewers for 5 minutes on each side.

Ingredients

6 boneless, skinless chicken thighs, cut into large thin sheets (about two pieces per thigh)

Marinade

2 cloves garlic, minced

1–2 hot chilies (such as Thai, serrano or jalapeños, depending on your preferred level of spiciness), minced

1 (1-inch) piece fresh ginger, peeled and minced

1/2 teaspoon dried turmeric

1 teaspoon ground coriander

1 teaspoon ground cumin

3 tablespoons soy sauce

3 tablespoons fish sauce

1/4 cup rice vinegar

A few drops sesame oil

1 tablespoon brown sugar

1/4 cup peanut butter

Directions

Combine marinade ingredients in a large bowl. Coat chicken in marinade; cover and refrigerate for 4 hours or overnight. The following day, soak skewers in water for 1 hour (weigh down with a plate to submerge). Preheat oven to 450 degrees. Place two pieces of chicken on each skewer. Place skewers on a baking sheet covered with aluminum foil and coated with canola oil. Bake chicken for 10 minutes, flip skewers and bake for an additional 20-25 minutes. Bake another 15 minutes, until chicken is brown and crisp on the edges. Serve hot or cold.

gfo: Use gluten-free varieties of soy sauce and fish sauce.

Serving suggestion: Serve with Fresh Spring Rolls (page 34).

Kefta Skewers (gf, df) Makes 8–10 skewers; entrée serves 4–6

Versions of this dish can be found from Bulgaria to Bangladesh. This one is probably closest to the Greek or Turkish style. Try spooning some Tzatziki Dip (page 27) into a pita and then sliding the kefta off the skewer to make a tasty sandwich.

Ingredients

1/4 cup sesame seeds

1/2 cup onion, shredded and excess water removed using a paper towel

2 garlic cloves, minced

1/4 teaspoon paprika

1/4 teaspoon black pepper

1/4 teaspoon ground cumin

1/8 teaspoon ground cayenne pepper

Pinch cinnamon

1 tablespoon parsley, minced

1/2 pound ground beef

1/2 pound ground pork

1 egg, beaten

1 tablespoon salt

Directions

Soak skewers in water for at least 30 minutes before cooking to prevent the wood from burning. Toast sesame seeds briefly in a dry pan over medium heat until they just start to pop. Combine all ingredients, except for salt, in a large bowl; mix with your hands until the mixture just comes together. Allow seasoned meat to rest in the refrigerator for at least 30 minutes and up to 24 hours. Preheat oven to 400 degrees. Form the chilled meat mixture into 6–8 tube shapes or oblong balls (each is called a kefta) before sliding a skewer lengthwise through each. Sprinkle each kefta generously with salt. Bake on a rack placed in a foil-lined baking pan for 10–20 minutes until skewers reach an internal temperature of 170 degrees. Cooking time will vary, depending on the shape of the kefta.

Serving suggestion: Serve in pita pockets with Tzatziki Dip (page 27).

Cantaloupe and Ham Skewers (gf, df) Makes 8–10 skewers

Salty, savory ham and sweet, juicy melon make a surprisingly delicious combination!

Ingredients

1–2 thick slices precooked ham steak, cut into 1- to 2-inch cubes

1 ripe cantaloupe, cut into bite-sized cubes

Directions

In a sauté pan over medium-high heat, quickly sear the cubed ham steak until the edges start to turn golden brown. Remove from heat and let cool until warm to the touch. Alternate placing pieces of ham and cantaloupe on skewers. Serve immediately, or refrigerate for several hours before serving.

Tropical Fruit Skewers (gf, v, df) Makes 8-10 skewers

Try these for a refreshing snack that offers a taste of the tropics on a hot summer day.

Ingredients

2-3 mangoes, cut into bite-sized pieces

1 pineapple, peeled, cored and cut into bite-sized pieces

1 pint blueberries

Directions

Alternate placing pieces of fruit on skewers.

Pimento Cheese Dip

Dips

tips to make serving easy

Serve these dips with chips, crackers or fresh veggies.

Serve each recipe in a heavy glass bowl or a baking dish to keep the dip and chips, crackers or veggies in place.

Place each glass serving dish on top of a silicone trivet on the table of the pontoon to prevent the dish from sliding.

Use rectangular paper food trays (which can be purchased online) for serving individual portions.

Each recipe in this section serves 6–8.

Chunky Salsa (gf, v, df) Makes about 1 pint

Salsa is the Spanish word for "sauce," and there are as many different salsas out there as there are cooks. In this book we present two salsa recipes perfect for dipping tortilla chips. This one is chunky and fresh with a mild, peppery zing.

Ingredients

3-4 large tomatoes, cored, seeded and finely chopped

1 clove garlic, minced

4-5 sprigs cilantro, minced

1/2 cup white onion, finely chopped

1 serrano or small jalapeño pepper, minced
  (adjust to preferred level of spiciness)

Juice from 1 lime

Salt and pepper

 Note: Taste salsa after combining all ingredients and add more lime juice, if necessary. Some tomatoes are sweeter than others and will need a little bit more lime juice.

Directions

In a large bowl, add tomatoes, garlic, cilantro, white onion, serrano chili and lime juice. Mix well. Add salt and pepper to taste. Serve with chips.

Roasted Tomatillo Salsa (gf, v, df) Makes about 1 pint

In contrast with the chunky salsa on page 18, this green salsa is smooth and tangy. Roasting the tomatillos gives it a slightly smoky flavor. Try it with frozen margaritas (page 73).

Ingredients

1/2 cup white onion, chopped

1 tablespoon canola or vegetable oil

5 medium tomatillos, husked and halved

2 cloves garlic, chopped

2 serrano chilies, chopped

1/3 cup fresh cilantro, chopped

Salt and white pepper

Directions

Place chopped onion into a small bowl. Cover with cold water and let sit for 15 minutes; drain. Add oil to a large shallow skillet over medium-high heat, and cook tomatillos, cut-side down, approximately 5 minutes. Turn tomatillos over and cook until soft (another 3-4 minutes). Remove tomatillos from pan and place in blender. Add garlic to pan over heat and cook for 30 seconds or until fragrant; remove from pan and add to blender along with tomatillos. Add onion, chilies and cilantro to blender; blend until smooth. Add salt and pepper to taste.

Guacamole (gf, v, df) Makes about 1 pint

This avocado-based dip has been popular since the time of the Aztecs, and for good reason! You will find that making your own guacamole from scratch is easy and a big improvement over store-bought varieties. Be sure to use ripe avocados: They should yield to the touch without being overly mushy. If you can't find any that are ripe yet, put a few into a paper bag and leave them on the kitchen counter. They should ripen in a day or two.

Ingredients

1/4 cup red or white onion, finely chopped

4 ripe avocados

Juice from 1 lime

8–10 sprigs fresh cilantro, minced

Salt and pepper

Directions

Place chopped onion into a small bowl. Cover with cold water and let sit for 15 minutes; drain. Cut each avocado in half; remove pit and scoop out flesh into a large bowl. Add onion, lime juice and cilantro. Mix well. Stir in salt and pepper to taste, adding more lime juice, if necessary. Serve with chips.

Roasted Tomatillo Guacamole (gf, v, df) Makes about 1 pint

A variation on classic guacamole, this version adds a smoky tang.

Ingredients

3 large avocados

1 recipe Roasted Tomatillo Salsa (page 19)

Salt and pepper to taste

Directions

Cut each avocado in half; remove pit and scrape out flesh into a large bowl. Stir in salsa. Season with salt and pepper to taste.

Yogurt-Feta Dip with Olives and Mint (gf, v)

Makes about 1 pint

This thick and tangy dip is great with cucumber slices or fresh veggies for dipping, but it also works well on crackers or French bread.

Ingredients

6 ounces feta

3/4 cup yogurt

1/4 cup fresh mint, chopped

1 tablespoon champagne vinegar

1 sprig oregano, chopped

1/8 teaspoon pepper

1 tablespoon olive oil

1/4 cup cream

Salt (optional)

10 Kalamata olives, finely chopped

Directions

Blend feta, yogurt, mint, vinegar, oregano, pepper and olive oil until well combined and mint is finely chopped. Stir in cream, adding more, if necessary, for blending. Stir in salt, if desired, and chopped olives. Serve cold.

Pimento Cheese (gf, v) Makes about 1 quart

A southern favorite, pimento cheese is becoming more and more popular across the rest of the U.S. Try this recipe and find out why! It's amazingly addictive on crackers or raw veggies.

Ingredients

3 cups cheddar cheese, shredded

8 ounces cream cheese, softened

1/2 cup mayonnaise

1/4 teaspoon garlic powder

1/4 teaspoon onion powder

1/4 teaspoon cayenne pepper

1 serrano or small jalapeño pepper, minced

1/4 teaspoon paprika

1 (4-ounce) jar diced pimentos, drained

Salt and pepper to taste

 Note: For best results and a gluten-free option, shred your own cheese. Many brands of shredded cheese contain wheat gluten.

For a creative touch:
Add 1/8 teaspoon smoked paprika.

Directions

Combine all ingredients in a large bowl.

Hummus (gf, v, df) Makes about 1 1/2 quarts per pound of dried chickpeas

We first started making our own hummus a few years ago and swore we'd never go back to the store-bought kind. A little time invested, and you'll have much better-tasting hummus at a fraction of the cost. Hummus freezes well and will last for months. Tahini is a sesame paste (like peanut butter, but with sesame seeds) that can be found in the international aisle of most grocery stores. Don't take shortcuts with canned chickpeas! The secret to great hummus is freshly preparing it from dried beans. Three flavor variations are given below. You can experiment with adding different herbs or vegetables, as long as the ingredients are soft enough to puree in a food processor.

Ingredients

To Prepare Chickpeas

1 pound dried chickpeas

1 carrot, broken into large pieces

2 celery stalks, broken into large pieces

1/2 onion, halved

To Prepare Hummus

3 cups cooked chickpeas

3/4 cup tahini

1 1/2 tablespoons lemon juice (about half a lemon)

1 1/2 teaspoons salt

1 cup olive oil

1/4 cup fresh parsley

1 teaspoon onion powder

1/2 teaspoon garlic powder

Pepper to taste

Directions

Prepare Chickpeas: Soak chickpeas overnight in water. The following day, strain chickpeas; add to a slow cooker with carrot, celery and onion. Add water to cover by 1 inch. Cook on high for 4 hours. Let chickpeas cool to room temperature. Discard carrot, celery and onion; strain chickpeas to remove excess water.

Prepare Hummus: Blend 3 cups cooked chickpeas with remaining ingredients in a food processor. If the hummus is too thick, stir in additional olive oil and lemon juice. Add more salt to taste, if necessary.

Flavor Variations

Tomato-Infused Hummus

Add 4 ounces tomato paste before processing.

Roasted Garlic Hummus

Take a whole head of garlic and, with a serrated knife, chop the top of the head off so that most of the cloves are exposed. Sprinkle with salt and olive oil before wrapping loosely in foil and roasting at 500 degrees for about 15 minutes. The skin should start to blacken and the garlic cloves should be very soft. Allow the garlic to cool before squeezing out the roasted garlic into your hummus mixture.

Hummus with Fresh Herbs

Add 1/4 cup fresh basil and 2 tablespoons fresh oregano (or 1 teaspoon dry).

Roasted Red Pepper Hummus

Roast a whole red pepper at 500 degrees for 10-15 minutes until the skin blisters and blackens. Allow the pepper to cool before running it under tap water while rubbing the skin gently to remove the blackened parts. Remove the stems and seeds before blending into the hummus.

 Note: A full pound of dry chickpeas will yield a quart and a half of hummus. If desired, split plain hummus into portions and make several different flavors. Or use some of the remaining chickpeas to make Falafel (page 40). Cooked chickpeas also store well in the freezer for future use.

Homemade Ranch (gf, v) Makes about 1 pint

Try this healthy homemade version and never go back to the store-bought kind!

Ingredients

1 cup mayonnaise

1/4 cup buttermilk

1/2 cup sour cream

1/4 teaspoon salt

1/3 cup fresh parsley, minced

1 tablespoon fresh dill, minced

1/4 cup fresh chives, minced

1/2 teaspoon black pepper

1/2 teaspoon lemon juice

1/4 teaspoon paprika

Directions

Combine all ingredients in a large bowl. For best results, let sit in the refrigerator for a few hours before serving. Serve cold.

Tzatziki Dip (gf, v) Makes about 3 cups

This popular Greek dish, somewhere between a condiment and a salad, goes with almost anything but is particularly tasty with Falafel (page 40) or Kefta Skewers (page 13). For a nice thick consistency, it is important to use "Greek" strained yogurt. If that is unavailable in your area, put a quart of plain, unsweetened yogurt into a fine sieve and allow it to drain into a large bowl in the refrigerator overnight. You can discard the whey or use it in place of buttermilk when baking.

Ingredients

1 cucumber, peeled and chopped

2 cups plain Greek yogurt

1 teaspoon fresh mint, finely chopped

2 teaspoons fresh parsley, finely chopped

1 1/2 tablespoons lemon juice (about half a lemon)

1/4 teaspoon garlic powder

Salt and pepper to taste

Directions

Combine all ingredients in a large bowl. Serve cold.

Caponata (gf, df) Makes about 1 quart

Caponata is a traditional Sicilian dish that can be enjoyed as a side item or as a topping for pasta, sandwiches, burgers or almost anything you can think of. Don't be afraid of the anchovies! They cook down into the mixture and provide a deep savory flavor without overpowering the other ingredients.

Ingredients

1 medium eggplant (1/2 to 3/4 pound)

Salt and pepper

1/4 cup pine nuts

1/2 green bell pepper, chopped

1 medium-size yellow onion, chopped (about 1 cup)

1/2 cup olive oil

3 cloves garlic, minced

3 anchovy fillets, minced

1 tablespoon tomato paste

1/2 cup dry red wine

1 (14-ounce) can diced tomatoes or 1 large tomato, peeled and chopped

2 tablespoons capers, rinsed and drained

1/4 cup green olives, sliced

1/4 cup Kalamata olives, sliced

2 tablespoons fresh basil (or 1 tablespoon dried)

1/4 cup fresh parsley, chopped

Note: This recipe can easily be doubled. Just increase the time that the eggplant and tomato mixture simmers to about 30 minutes. Hot caponata packed into clean Mason jars and refrigerated will keep for up to a few weeks.

Directions

Peel eggplant and cut into 1/2-inch cubes. Salt eggplant liberally and place in a colander or paper towel-lined bowl to drain. Meanwhile, toast pine nuts in a dry pan over medium-low heat, tossing frequently until fragrant and beginning to brown slightly, about 5 minutes. Set aside. Sauté bell pepper and onion in olive oil over medium-high heat in a large heavy skillet. (It will seem like a lot of olive oil at first, until all of the remaining ingredients are added.) Continue cooking until onion turns translucent and starts to brown slightly around the edges, about 10-15 minutes. Add garlic, anchovies, tomato paste and eggplant; continue to cook for an additional 10-15 minutes. Deglaze pan with wine, and add tomatoes along with their juices. Simmer for about 20 minutes to reduce, stirring occasionally. The final consistency should be quite thick and not at all runny. Remove from heat; add capers, olives, herbs and pine nuts. Season with salt and pepper to taste. Serve with crusty French bread or crackers.

Layered Greek Dip (gf, v) Makes 8–10 servings

This is a cool Mediterranean twist on a traditional seven-layer dip.

Ingredients

2 cups hummus (tomato-infused version on page 25 or store-bought)

2 cups plain Greek yogurt

2 tablespoons Greek seasoning herb blend

Juice from half a lemon (about 1 1/2 tablespoons)

Salt and pepper

1 cucumber, peeled, seeds removed and chopped

1 cup canned black olives, sliced

1/2 red bell pepper, chopped

1 bunch scallions, chopped

4 ounces feta, crumbled

Note: If you cannot find an herb blend of Greek seasoning, you can substitute 1/2 tablespoon each dried basil, oregano, parsley and onion powder.

Directions

Layer hummus evenly over bottom of a square 8- x 8-inch dish, spreading well into corners of dish. In a medium bowl, combine yogurt, Greek seasoning, lemon juice, salt and pepper. Add more seasoning to taste, if necessary. Layer yogurt mixture evenly over hummus layer. Sprinkle cucumber, black olives, red bell pepper, scallions and feta evenly over yogurt. Chill until ready to serve. Serve with tortilla chips or crackers.

Olive and Sun-Dried Tomato Tapenade (gf, v, df)

Makes about 1 quart

Quick to make, this flavorful, Mediterranean-inspired topping is best enjoyed with crackers
or on slices of toast or French bread. Try serving it alongside the Antipasto Skewers on page 8.

Ingredients

2 cloves garlic, cut in half

1/4 cup capers

2 cups canned black olives, sliced

1/2 cup green olives stuffed with
pimentos, sliced

1/2 cup celery, sliced (about 1 stalk)

1/3 cup sun-dried tomatoes, sliced

1/2 tablespoon red wine vinegar

2 teaspoons dried oregano

1/3 cup high-quality olive oil

Directions

Blend all ingredients together in a food processor.

Asparagus Wrapped in Prosciutto

Finger Foods

tips to make serving easy

Serve finger foods in a portable shallow container, such as a heavy glass dish or a plastic container. Or arrange them on large serving trays, and then place the trays on silicone trivets to prevent sliding.

A spray bottle filled with water and a roll of paper towels make cleanup of sticky fingers a breeze and eliminate the worry of polluting the lake with soap.

Many of these recipes can be combined with recipes from other chapters to make complete meals.

Each recipe in this section serves 6–8.

Fresh Spring Rolls (gfo, v, df) Makes 10 spring rolls

Fresh spring rolls are a healthy snack and fun to make, once you get the hang of it.
Cucumbers and mint make for a cooling treat on a hot day.

Ingredients

1 cup smooth peanut butter

2 tablespoons soy sauce

1 1/2 tablespoons Sriracha

2 tablespoons rice vinegar

1-2 tablespoons water

1 teaspoon fresh ginger, finely grated

1 small clove garlic, finely grated

1/2 teaspoon sesame oil

1/2 package vermicelli noodles
(found in the international section of the grocery store)

8 spring roll wrappers (rice)

6 ounces baby spinach

1/2 cucumber, seeds scooped out and cut into thin strips

1 carrot, shredded

1/2 cup crushed roasted peanuts (optional)

1/2 cup scallions, sliced

1 bunch fresh cilantro

Small handful fresh mint

1 lime

Hoisin sauce for dipping (optional)

Directions

In a medium bowl, combine peanut butter, soy sauce, Sriracha, rice vinegar, water, ginger, garlic and sesame oil until well mixed. Set aside. Cook noodles for 3 minutes in boiling water. Strain, and rinse with cool water to prevent further cooking and to reduce stickiness. Set aside. Heat a gallon of water until hot to the touch (not boiling) to soften the spring roll wrappers.

To assemble spring rolls (see diagram below), dip a spring roll wrapper into hot water until completely coated. Remove from water and place onto a large plate. The wrapper will begin to soften and become pliable and sticky. Place a small handful of spinach in the center of the wrap. Spread 2 tablespoons peanut butter mixture on top of spinach. On top of peanut butter mixture, layer roughly 1/4 cup noodles, a few cucumber strips, some shredded carrot, peanuts, scallions, a few sprigs cilantro (stems removed), two mint leaves and a small squeeze of lime juice. Wrap the spring roll by folding over one side of the wrapper to just cover the filling ingredients; fold each opposite side toward the middle over the filling about 2 inches. Then, holding the ends in, wrap the spring roll up. Serve immediately or chill for up to 2 hours before serving.

gfo: Use gluten-free spring roll wrappers, vermicelli noodles and soy sauce, and omit the hoisin sauce.

Serving suggestion: Serve alongside Chicken Satay Skewers (page 12).

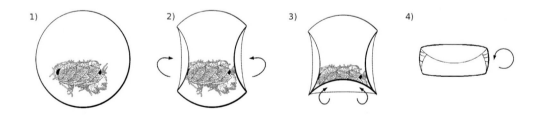

1)   2)   3)   4)

Asparagus Wrapped in Prosciutto (gf, df)

Makes 8–10 appetizer servings

Visually attractive, easy to make and even more fun to eat, this elegant dish is simply wonderful!

Ingredients

1 bunch asparagus, ends trimmed

1 1/2 tablespoons lemon juice (about 1/2 a lemon)

Salt and pepper to taste

4 ounces prosciutto, sliced into quarters (approximately 4- x 2-inch sheets)

Directions

Steam asparagus for about 1 minute or until stalks turn bright green and just begin to become tender. Remove from heat and rinse with cold water to prevent overcooking. Toss asparagus in lemon juice, salt and pepper. Wrap the bottom of each asparagus spear in a quarter of a prosciutto slice. Serve cold.

Bacon-Wrapped Dates (gf, df) Makes 24 bite-sized pieces

These are sometimes called "devils on horseback," though no one seems to know why. Maybe it's because the perfect combination of sweet dates and savory bacon sure feels a little sinful!

Ingredients

24 toothpicks

24 dates

1 pound bacon strips, cut into quarters

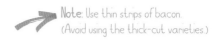 Note: Use thin strips of bacon.
(Avoid using the thick-cut varieties.)

Directions

Soak toothpicks in water 15–20 minutes. Preheat oven to 425 degrees. Wrap each date with a piece of bacon, secure with a toothpick and place on a wire rack over a rimmed foil-lined baking sheet. Bake 10–12 minutes or until bacon is thoroughly cooked and crispy.

For a creative touch:

Try stuffing each date with a pistachio.

Lox on Toasted Bagel Points Makes 48 small bites

Smoky salmon and the smooth richness of cream cheese are perfectly complemented by tangy capers and the mild bite of chopped red onion. These are great for brunch with a cup of good coffee (or a glass of champagne!).

Ingredients

4 plain bagels

8 ounces cream cheese, softened

1/2 cup red onion, finely chopped

1/2 cup capers, coarsely chopped

6 ounces smoked salmon

Note: Be sure to keep these cold while on the boat until it's time to serve them. We find that soft, prepackaged bagels work best for this recipe.

Directions

Cut bagels in half and toast. Let bagels cool, and cut into sixths. Spread toasted bagel points evenly with cream cheese; sprinkle with red onion and capers, and layer with smoked salmon. Serve cold.

For a creative touch:

Try using different flavors of bagels, such as "everything" or "poppy seed."

Grilled Caesar Salad (gf) Makes 6 servings

You might not think a salad would make a great pontoon snack, but this preparation is both delicious and easy to eat. The romaine hearts are split lengthwise and brushed with a thick dressing, so they can be eaten with your fingers, mess free.

Ingredients

2 tablespoons olive oil

1 1/2 tablespoons balsamic vinegar

3 small romaine hearts, cut in half lengthwise, leaving the bottom stem intact

 Note: It is important to add the olive oil and balsamic vinegar to a cold pan and then increase the heat, to prevent the vinegar from spattering.

Dressing

1 clove garlic, minced

1 anchovy (or pickled herring) fillet

1 tablespoon lemon juice

1 teaspoon Dijon mustard

1 teaspoon Worcestershire

1 cup mayonnaise

1/2 cup Parmesan cheese, shredded

1/4 teaspoon salt

1/4 teaspoon pepper

Directions

In a large shallow skillet, add olive oil and balsamic vinegar, and heat over medium-high heat. Once skillet is hot, quickly sauté each romaine half, flat side down, for approximately 1 minute or until romaine starts to develop some color (but before romaine starts to wilt).

In a small food processor, blend garlic, anchovy, lemon juice, mustard and Worcestershire. In a small bowl, combine mayonnaise, Parmesan, salt and pepper; stir in anchovy mixture.

To serve, place grilled romaine hearts in a plastic container or on a serving platter, flat side up, and brush liberally with dressing. To eat, use the bottom stem portion of the dressed romaine heart as a handle.

Falafel (gfo, v, df) Makes about 1 dozen

One of civilization's original street foods, falafel was popular among travelers along ancient spice-trading routes and incorporated faraway flavors, such as cumin, coriander and black pepper. Later, falafel became an important staple of early Christians as a meat substitute during Lent. Try it with Tzatziki Dip (page 27).

Ingredients

1 (15-ounce) can chickpeas, mashed

1 teaspoon sesame seeds

1 onion, coarsely chopped (about 2 cups)

1/2 cup fresh parsley, coarsely chopped

3 cloves garlic, coarsely chopped

1 tablespoon olive oil

1 egg

1 teaspoon ground cumin

1 teaspoon ground coriander

1 teaspoon salt

1/2 teaspoon pepper

1/4 teaspoon cayenne pepper

1 teaspoon lemon juice

1/4 teaspoon lemon zest

1 teaspoon baking powder

1 cup breadcrumbs

Vegetable or canola oil

Directions

Drain and rinse chickpeas. In a large bowl, mash chickpeas with a potato masher (do not blend). Briefly toast sesame seeds in a small pan over medium-high heat for about 30 seconds. Remove from heat and set aside. In a blender, combine onion, parsley and garlic; blend until smooth. In a large bowl, combine chickpeas, onion mixture and olive oil. In a small bowl, combine egg, cumin, coriander, salt, pepper, cayenne, lemon juice, lemon zest, baking powder and toasted sesame seeds; mix well. Add egg mixture to chickpea mixture until combined. Slowly add 3/4 cup breadcrumbs. If necessary, gradually add more breadcrumbs until mixture holds together enough to form into balls about the size of doughnut holes. Heat 1–2 inches of oil in a large shallow skillet until oil reaches 350 degrees. Fry balls, in batches, about 5-6 minutes or until brown and golden on all sides.

gfo: Use gluten-free breadcrumbs.

Stuffed Mushrooms (gfo, v) Makes about 20 stuffed pieces

Impress your guests with these fancy-looking bites that are actually pretty easy to make. They can be enjoyed cold, but they are best served warm.

Ingredients

16 ounces fresh mushrooms (white button or cremini)

1/2 cup onion, finely chopped

3 tablespoons olive oil

1 clove garlic, minced

1 1/2 tablespoons lemon juice (about half a lemon)

1/3 cup panko-style breadcrumbs

1/2 cup Romano cheese, freshly shredded or grated

1/4 cup fresh parsley, finely chopped

Salt and pepper to taste

Note: Mushrooms can be stuffed up to a day or two ahead of time and stored in the refrigerator. Roast just before serving.

Directions

Preheat oven to 425 degrees. Separate mushroom caps and stems, setting the caps aside. Dice the mushroom stems and reserve. Over medium-high heat, sauté onion in olive oil. When onion becomes soft and translucent (about 5 minutes), add chopped mushroom stems; sauté until stems expel juices, about 5–10 minutes. Add garlic and lemon juice, and cook a few more minutes until most of the liquid has evaporated. Remove mixture from heat and allow to cool slightly. Mix in breadcrumbs, cheese and parsley. Season with salt and pepper. Stuff mushroom caps with breadcrumb mixture. If stuffing is too dry, add more olive oil. Arrange stuffed mushrooms on a parchment paper-lined baking sheet and roast for 10 minutes or until mushroom caps are soft and stuffing begins to brown.

gfo: Use gluten-free breadcrumbs.

Apple Wedges with Blue Cheese and Prosciutto (gf)

Makes about 20 bites

This is like a fancy cheese plate packaged into perfect little bites. Sweet-tart Granny Smith apples pair perfectly with salty cured ham and funky blue cheese. Try this treat as an appetizer or a dessert.

Ingredients

1 Granny Smith apple, sliced

Juice from half a lemon (about 2 tablespoons)

4 ounces blue cheese, sliced into bite-sized rectangles

4 ounces prosciutto, sliced into quarters (approximately 4- x 2-inch sheets)

Directions

Toss apple slices with lemon juice. Top each apple slice with a piece of blue cheese. Wrap each apple-and-blue cheese wedge with a quarter slice of prosciutto. Serve cold.

Twice-Baked Potato Skins (gf) Makes 8 appetizer servings

With this recipe, you can enjoy the classic flavors of fully loaded baked potatoes on the go. No forks or knives required!

Ingredients

4 Russet potatoes

2 cups cheddar cheese, shredded

1 bunch scallions, chopped

6 slices bacon, fried, cooled and crumbled

3/4 cup sour cream or plain Greek yogurt

1/2 cup milk

Salt and pepper to taste

Directions

Preheat oven to 425 degrees. Thoroughly rinse potatoes. Place potatoes on a baking sheet, and prick each potato with a knife to release steam during cooking. Bake potatoes until cooked completely through (about an hour to an hour and a half). Let potatoes cool enough to handle. Cut each potato in half lengthwise, and scoop out flesh of each half into a large bowl, reserving skins. Add 1 1/2 cups cheese, scallions, bacon, sour cream, milk, salt and pepper; mix thoroughly. Adjust potato mixture to desired thickness by adding more sour cream and/or milk. Taste potato mixture and adjust seasoning, if desired. Place empty skins onto a baking sheet, and fill skins with potato mixture. Bake potato skins at 375 degrees for 15 minutes; top with remaining cheese, and bake for an additional 5–10 minutes or until tops start to turn golden brown. To serve, cut each baked potato skin in half. Serve hot or cold.

gfo: Use gluten-free brands of shredded cheese, bacon and sour cream.

Stuffed Artichoke Bottoms (gf, v) Makes about 8-10 bites

Sometimes overlooked by cooks, tender artichoke bottoms pack a ton of flavor. Dressed with flavorful stuffing and fresh mozzarella, these tasty bites are best served warm.

Ingredients

1 (14-ounce) can artichoke bottoms

2 tablespoons shallot, minced

2 cloves garlic, minced

3-4 mushrooms (any kind), minced

1/4 cup red bell pepper, diced

Olive oil

Salt and pepper

2-3 basil leaves, minced

2 tablespoons parsley, minced

4 ounces fresh mozzarella, sliced into 8-10 rounds

Directions

Drain artichoke bottoms and place onto a parchment paper-lined baking sheet. In a large skillet, sauté shallot, garlic, mushrooms and red bell pepper in oil over medium heat until mushrooms become tender, about 10-15 minutes. Season with salt and pepper; stir in basil and parsley. Place large dollops of stuffing mixture on top of artichoke bottoms. Place one slice of mozzarella cheese over each stuffed artichoke bottom. Sprinkle with salt and pepper. Broil 5-7 minutes or until mozzarella becomes brown and bubbly.

Spicy Tortilla Pinwheels (v) Makes about 40 pinwheel bites

These tortilla bites can be made ahead and brought out for an afternoon snack or an appetizer at happy hour.

Ingredients

3–4 scallions, coarsely chopped

1 serrano or jalapeño pepper, seeds removed and coarsely chopped

1/4 red bell pepper, coarsely chopped

Handful of cilantro

8 ounces cream cheese, softened

4 ounces pimentos, diced

4 ounces black olives, diced

2 tablespoons hot sauce

Pinch of salt

6–8 large flour tortillas

Note: These can turn out quite spicy, depending on the peppers that you use. To reduce spiciness, reduce hot sauce to 1 tablespoon and add an additional 1/8 teaspoon salt.

For a creative touch: Try using different flavors of hot sauce or different varieties of peppers.

Directions

Combine scallions, chili pepper, red bell pepper and cilantro in a food processor, and blend until ingredients are finely chopped; transfer to a large bowl. Stir in cream cheese, pimentos, black olives, hot sauce and salt; mix until thoroughly combined. Taste mixture and add more salt, if needed. Spread a large spoonful of cream cheese mixture onto a tortilla, and roll the tortilla up. Repeat with remaining tortillas. Refrigerate at least 1 hour before cutting. Once chilled, cut tortilla rolls into 1 1/2-inch pinwheels. Serve cold.

New Potatoes Stuffed with Roasted Garlic-Chipotle Aioli (gf, v) Makes 8-10 appetizer servings

These are perfect potato bites, creamy but with a hint of smoky chipotle.

Ingredients

2 pounds small new or red potatoes, about the size of golf balls

2 tablespoons olive oil

Salt and pepper

1 large sprig rosemary

6 large cloves garlic

1 cup sour cream

1 ounce cream cheese, softened

2 tablespoons sauce from a can of chipotles in adobo sauce

1 teaspoon paprika

Salt and pepper to taste

2 tablespoons fresh chives, finely chopped

Directions

Preheat oven to 425 degrees. Wash potatoes well and pat dry. Place potatoes in a large glass baking dish, and coat potatoes with olive oil,

Note: If you like a bit more kick, add a whole chipotle, minced (from the can of chipotles in adobo sauce), to the aioli mixture.

pepper and a generous amount of salt (about 1 tablespoon). Add rosemary and 6 cloves garlic, in their skins, to the dish; put dish in oven. After 20 minutes or until garlic cloves are soft beneath their papery skin, remove garlic from pan, and set aside. Continue roasting potatoes until completely cooked through (approximately 15 to 25 more minutes), stirring potatoes occasionally. Once potatoes are completely cooked, remove from oven and allow to cool to room temperature. In the meantime, prepare the aioli by combining sour cream, cream cheese, chipotle, paprika and 1/4 teaspoon salt. Peel roasted garlic, mince, and add to aioli mixture. Taste aioli, and add salt and pepper, if necessary. Once potatoes are cool, scoop out a tablespoon of flesh from the top of each potato using a melon baller or a small spoon. Sprinkle a generous amount of salt and a little bit of pepper over potatoes before filling. Using the melon baller, place about 1 tablespoon aioli into each potato. For a cleaner look, place aioli into a small plastic zip-top bag; cut off the tip of one corner, and use it as a piping bag. If potatoes are rolling around and not sitting flat, use a knife to cut the bottoms of potatoes to make a flat surface. Top potatoes with finely chopped fresh chives. Place potatoes in a large plastic container, and refrigerate until ready to eat.

Faux-Monsieur Wrap

Sandwiches & Wraps

tips to make serving easy

For Sandwiches: The sandwich recipes in this chapter are designed for pita pockets, which are easier to pack and eat out on the water than sandwiches made with traditional breads. However, the recipes will work equally well on the bread of your choice. Take care not to split the bottom of the pita pocket when filling, to avoid any mess on the pontoon. For a gluten-free option, serve sandwich fillings in lettuce cups.

For Wraps: The wrap recipes yield about 4-6 rolled tortillas. Cut each rolled tortilla into 3- to 4-inch slices. You can use large rectangular tortillas for the most efficient use of surface area, but large round tortillas work just as well. For a creative touch, use spinach or other flavored tortillas.

These wraps are best made by layering the ingredients over 3/4 of the tortilla, leaving one edge of the tortilla free. When rolling, start with a side of the tortilla with ingredients, and roll toward the empty edge. This will help prevent some of the ingredients from sliding out of the finished wrap. These wraps can be made well in advance. Just be sure they are kept cold until time to serve.

Each recipe in this section serves 6-8.

Your Regular Ol' Pita Makes 6–8 servings

Sometimes classic is the only way to go. Ranch dressing adds a unique zing.

Ingredients

8 pita pockets (4 pitas cut in half)

8 slices sandwich meat of your choice, cut in half

8 slices cheese of your choice, cut in half

1/2 cup ranch dressing

Tomato slices

1/2 red onion, sliced

1/2 cucumber, peeled and cut into matchstick-sized pieces

2 cups baby spinach, coarsely chopped

Directions

In each pita pocket, add half of a slice of meat, top with half of a slice of cheese, drizzle with ranch and top with tomato, onion and cucumber slices. Add another half slice of meat and cheese, along with another drizzle of ranch and top with a few chopped spinach leaves.

Egg Salad Pita (v) Makes 6–8 servings

Cool, refreshing and hearty at the same time.

Ingredients

8 pita pockets (4 pitas cut in half)

8 eggs, hard-boiled

1/2 cup mayonnaise

1 tablespoon sharp mustard (such as Dijon or deli mustard)

1 teaspoon dried dill

1/4 teaspoon paprika

1/2 stalk celery, minced (optional)

Salt and pepper to taste

Directions

Peel eggs; coarsely chop and add to a large bowl with mayonnaise and next 5 ingredients. Mix well, and stuff into pita pockets.

Chicken Salad Pita with Golden Raisins Makes 6–8 servings

This is our absolute favorite way to make chicken salad. It's important to use roasted chicken, if you can. Pick up a rotisserie chicken from the grocery store, or roast a chicken for dinner and use the leftovers to make chicken salad for lunch the next day.

Ingredients

8 pita pockets (4 pitas cut in half)

3 cups roasted chicken (skin removed), cubed

1 large green apple, peeled and chopped

1/2 cup golden raisins

1/2 cup pecans, toasted and chopped

1 tablespoon fresh tarragon, minced

1 1/4 cups mayonnaise

2 tablespoons rice vinegar

1/4 teaspoon lemon zest

Salt and pepper to taste

Directions

In a large bowl, combine chicken, apples, raisins, pecans and tarragon. In a small bowl, combine mayonnaise, vinegar and lemon zest. Add salt and pepper to taste. Add mayonnaise mixture to chicken mixture, and toss to coat. Refrigerate for at least 1 hour before stuffing into pita pockets.

Falafel Pita (v) Makes 6–8 servings

Falafel is not only a great finger food, but it's also delicious in sandwiches. These pita sandwiches make a tasty and hearty vegetarian meal.

Ingredients

8 pita pockets (4 pitas cut in half)

Falafel (page 40)

1 cup plain Greek yogurt or Tzatziki Dip (page 27)

1/2 red onion, sliced

1 tomato, sliced

1 cucumber, peeled and sliced

Directions

Prepare Falafel as directed. In each pita pocket, place 2–3 Falafel balls. Top Falafel with yogurt, red onion, tomato and cucumber slices.

Faux-Monsieur Wrap Makes 6–8 servings

The croque-monsieur sandwich originated in French cafés around the turn of the twentieth century. On a cold and rainy day, a hot croque-monsieur covered in melted cheese is a wonderful thing. These wraps are a riff on the flavor profile of that hot sandwich, served cold for warm days by the water.

Ingredients

4 large tortillas

1/2 cup strawberry jam

1/2 pound ham deli meat, sliced

1/4 cup spicy mustard

1 cup Gruyère cheese, shredded

1 cup arugula

For a creative touch:

Try substituting lingonberry jam for strawberry jam or adding sliced banana peppers to add a little more crunch.

Directions

Spread jam on each tortilla. Layer with ham, mustard, shredded Gruyère and arugula. Roll each tortilla into a tight wrap, and cut into 3- to 4-inch slices. Serve cold.

Mediterranean Wrap (v) Makes 6–8 servings

Light and healthy, the hummus and feta cheese give this wrap enough weight to be really satisfying.

Ingredients

4 large tortillas

1 cup Tomato-Infused Hummus (page 25)
or a store-bought variety

1 cup Tzatziki Dip (page 27)

2 carrots, grated

1/2 red onion, sliced

1/2 cup Kalamata olives, diced

2 ounces feta cheese, crumbled

2 cups baby spinach

Directions

On a large tortilla, spread evenly with a thin layer of hummus, followed by a thin layer of Tzatziki Dip. Top with grated carrots, red onion, Kalamata olives, feta cheese and a single layer of spinach leaves. Roll the tortilla into a tight wrap and cut into 3- to 4-inch slices. Serve cold.

NOLA Wrap
Makes 6–8 servings

The muffuletta (pronounced muff-uh-lot-a) sandwich is one of the signature flavors of New Orleans. Invented in the French Quarter's Central Grocery, the muffuletta sandwich has gained fame worldwide. Enjoy these yummy wraps based on the flavors of the Big Easy classic.

Ingredients

4 large tortillas

8 ounces cream cheese, softened

1 cup Olive and Sun-dried Tomato Tapenade (page 31) or store-bought

1/4 pound ham deli meat, sliced

1/4 pound Genoa salami, sliced

8 ounces provolone, sliced

8 pepperoncini, sliced

Directions

Spread cream cheese and olive tapenade evenly on each tortilla. Layer with ham, salami and provolone. Sprinkle with pepperoncini. Roll each tortilla into a tight wrap, and cut into 3- to 4-inch slices.

Brownie Cupcakes with Molten Caramel, Fresh Fruit Skewers, Peanut Butter Chocolate Chip Cookies

Sweets

tips to make serving easy

Be sure to pack along some napkins for these finger-licking-good desserts. Pack napkins in a large plastic bag with a heavy object inside—such as a large metal spoon—to prevent the napkins from blowing away.

Each of our half-pint sweets recipes—Cheesecake with Fresh Berry Compote, Buttermilk Panna Cotta and Butterscotch Pudding—yields approximately 8 half-pint jars.

Half-pint jelly jars are a convenient and fun way to take dessert with you. Alternatively, for the Panna Cotta and Butterscotch Pudding, you may use disposable cups and cover them with plastic wrap.

Each recipe in this section serves 8.

Puppy Chow (gf, v) Makes about a full gallon zip-top bag

The recipe name comes from its appearance, but there's no mistaking these perfect little bites of crispy, chocolate-and-peanut buttery goodness.

Ingredients

2 cups semisweet chocolate chips (1 [12-ounce] bag)

1/2 cup butter, melted

3/4 cup peanut butter, smooth

1 box rice cereal squares (12 ounces)

2 cups powdered sugar

Directions

In a medium saucepan over low heat, melt chocolate chips along with the already melted butter (this will prevent the chocolate from seizing up during melting). Add peanut butter and stir until well combined. In a very large bowl, combine rice cereal squares and melted chocolate mixture. Mix gently with a rubber spatula to avoid breaking the rice cereal squares. (This takes a little patience, but it will come together eventually.) Once cereal is completely coated, place about a quarter of the rice cereal mixture into a large plastic bag along with 1/2 cup powdered sugar. Seal the bag and shake gently until all of the rice cereal is evenly coated. Carefully remove coated rice cereal and place into a separate plastic container. Continue to add batches of chocolate-coated rice cereal and 1/2 cup powdered sugar until all cereal is coated. Serve at room temperature.

No-Bake Cookies (gfo, v) Makes about 2 dozen cookies

These are terrific on warm summer days when you'd rather not heat up the kitchen with a hot oven. This recipe doesn't require knives, so it's also a great way for young kids to join in the fun of cooking.

Ingredients

2 cups sugar

1/4 cup cocoa powder

1/2 cup butter (1 stick)

1/2 cup milk

1/2 cup peanut butter, smooth

2 cups rolled oats

1 cup peanuts

 Note: Keep cookies in the cooler until ready to eat.

Directions

In a large saucepan, stir together sugar, cocoa, butter and milk. Bring to a boil and remove from heat. Stir in peanut butter, oats and peanuts. Allow to cool in pan for 5–10 minutes. Line a baking sheet with parchment paper, and drop spoonfuls of chocolate-oat mixture onto baking sheet. Refrigerate for at least 4 hours or until cookies are firm. Serve cold.

gfo: Use gluten-free oats.

Peanut Butter Chocolate Chip Cookies (gfo, v)

Makes about 20 cookies

Erin has been perfecting this recipe for years; the best part is, you only have to get one bowl dirty to make these cookies! Be careful not to overcook them: They should not be fully set when you remove them from the oven.

Ingredients

1/2 cup smooth peanut butter

1/2 cup butter, softened

1 egg

1 1/4 cups flour

1/2 cup sugar

1/2 cup brown sugar

1/2 teaspoon baking powder

1/2 teaspoon baking soda

1/2 teaspoon vanilla

1 cup semisweet chocolate chips

Directions

Preheat oven to 375 degrees. In a large bowl, blend together peanut butter and butter. Add egg, 1/2 cup flour, sugars, baking powder, baking soda and vanilla. Mix until just combined. Slowly add remaining flour. Fold in chocolate chips. Roll into small balls and press slightly with a fork. Bake until just starting to brown (about 8 minutes). Remove cookies from oven but leave on baking sheet for another 4–5 minutes or until cookies firm up. Place cookies on cooling rack until completely cool.

gfo: Use a gluten-free all-purpose flour mixture.

Brownie Cupcakes with Molten Caramel (gfo, v)

Makes 1 dozen cupcakes

These rich and chewy brownies contain a hidden surprise.

Ingredients

1 box chocolate brownie mix

12 cupcake liners

12 caramel squares (or other bite-sized candy pieces, such as peanut butter cups or caramel-filled chocolates), unwrapped

Note: These mixes typically call for additional ingredients, such as eggs, butter or oil, so read the directions of the mix that you are using and be sure to get the additional ingredients that it calls for.

Directions

Preheat oven to 350 degrees. Follow package directions on brownie mix to make the batter. Place cupcake liners in a muffin tin; pour batter evenly into cupcake liners, filling about 2/3 of the way up. Bake cupcakes for 7–8 minutes or until about halfway cooked. Remove cupcakes from oven, and place a caramel (or candy piece) into the center of each cupcake. Place cupcakes back in the oven for another 10–12 minutes or until cupcakes are completely cooked through and caramel is melted. Serve warm.

gfo: Use a gluten-free brownie mix.

Cracker Candy (gfo, v)
Makes 8 servings

This recipe is super simple and uses only 5 ingredients, but it just might be the most delicious and addictive toffee candy you've ever tasted.

Ingredients

1/2 pound butter (2 sticks), plus more for greasing pan

1 (16-ounce) package saltine crackers

3/4 cup sugar

2 cups semisweet chocolate chips

3/4 cup chopped walnuts or pecans

Directions

Preheat oven to 425 degrees. Line a baking sheet with aluminum foil and grease liberally with butter. Arrange saltines in a single layer on foil-lined baking sheet. Melt butter in a saucepan over medium heat. When butter is melted, add sugar to pan and bring to a low boil. Boil for 3 minutes, stirring and scraping constantly with a wooden spoon to prevent burning. Carefully pour butter-sugar mixture over crackers, and bake for 5 minutes. Remove from oven, and sprinkle chocolate chips evenly over the top. As chips melt, use a rubber spatula to spread chocolate into an even layer. Sprinkle chopped nuts over top. Cool in the refrigerator until chocolate has fully hardened, at least 1 hour. Remove candy from foil and break into pieces. Store in refrigerator or cooler until ready to eat.

gfo: Use gluten-free matzo-style crackers instead of saltines.

Fresh Fruit Skewers (gf, v, df) Makes 8-10 skewers

Simple and straightforward, delicious fresh fruit is hard to beat as a healthy snack or a dessert.

Ingredients

1 pint blackberries, rinsed and drained

2 peaches, rinsed, peeled and cut into bite-sized pieces

1 pound fresh strawberries, rinsed and cut into bite-sized pieces

4 fresh kiwis, rinsed, peeled and cut into bite-sized pieces

Directions

Alternate placing fruit on skewers.

Cheesecake with Fresh Berry Compote (v)

Makes 8 individual servings

Here is a real, made-from-scratch cheesecake with graham cracker crust and fresh berries, in individual portions.

Ingredients

3/4 cup graham cracker crumbs

1/3 cup pecans, toasted and finely chopped

2 tablespoons sugar

1/3 cup butter, melted

8 pint-size, ovenproof glass jars with lids

3 (8-ounce) packages cream cheese, softened

3/4 cup sugar

3 eggs

1 teaspoon vanilla extract

2 pints fresh berries (blueberries, raspberries, blackberries and/or strawberries), rinsed and drained

1/4 cup sugar

1/2 tablespoon orange liqueur, such as Cointreau (optional)

For a creative touch:
Substitute a quarter of a fresh vanilla bean for vanilla extract.

Directions

Preheat oven to 350 degrees. Combine graham cracker crumbs, pecans, sugar and melted butter in a large mixing bowl. Line the bottom of each jar with a half-inch layer of crust mixture, and pack down crust completely. (This is done easiest with a muddler.) Place jars onto a large rimmed baking sheet, and bake for 10–12 minutes or until crusts begin to brown slightly. Combine cream cheese and sugar using a mixer. Add eggs (one at a time) along with vanilla. Mix until well combined, but do not overmix. Pour batter equally into each jar, filling jars 3/4 full. Carefully wipe off any cream cheese mixture that may have spilled on sides of jars. Fill baking dish with 1–2 inches hot water; place jars in dish, and bake cheesecakes at 350 degrees for 25–30 minutes or until filling is set completely. Meanwhile, combine fresh berries, sugar and, if desired, Cointreau. When cheesecakes are completely cooked, remove from oven and let cool to room temperature. Cover jars with lids and store in the fridge for 4 hours (or overnight). Top with berry compote before serving. Replace lids and store in a cooler until ready to eat.

Buttermilk Panna Cotta with Candied Pistachios (gf)

Makes 8 individual servings

Custardy and rich, the tartness of the buttermilk in this recipe is tempered with sugar and candied nuts.

Ingredients

4 cups buttermilk

3 1/2 teaspoons unflavored gelatin

2 cups heavy cream

1 cup sugar

2 teaspoons vanilla extract

Salt

8 pint-size, ovenproof glass jars with lids

1 cup pistachios, shelled

2 tablespoons honey

1 tablespoon sugar

Directions

Note: Use high-quality, full-fat buttermilk, if available. It's also important to do the straining step to remove any undissolved gelatin; otherwise, the panna cotta will become grainy.

In a large saucepan, add 2 cups buttermilk; sprinkle with gelatin. Let gelatin; rehydrate for 5 minutes before stirring to combine. In a medium saucepan, bring cream and 1 cup sugar to a gentle boil. Remove from heat; slowly stir into buttermilk-gelatin mixture. Whisk buttermilk-cream mixture over low heat until gelatin is completely dissolved (about 5-7 minutes). Remove from heat, and strain through a sieve into a large bowl to remove any undissolved gelatin particles. Add remaining buttermilk, vanilla and pinch of salt to bowl; stir to combine. Pour panna cotta mixture evenly into each jar until about 2/3 full. Cover each jar with a lid and very carefully move to the fridge to chill for at least 4 hours or overnight. Meanwhile, in a large bowl, combine pistachios, honey, 1 tablespoon sugar and pinch of salt; mix until nuts are evenly coated. Spread nuts in a thin layer on a parchment paper-lined baking sheet; bake at 350 degrees for 6-8 minutes. Remove nuts from oven; cool. When jars of panna cotta are set, top each jar with a layer of candied pistachios.

For a creative touch: Substitute half of a fresh vanilla bean for vanilla extract, or add 1-2 drops of rose water to the buttermilk mixture before pouring into jars.

Butterscotch Pudding (gf, v) Makes 8 individual servings

A classic dessert that, sadly, isn't seen much these days, it's simple to make with common and affordable ingredients—in fact, you might have the ingredients in your pantry already. The "scotch" part of the name probably does not come from Scotch whisky, but it rather refers to the process of making butterscotch candy, either from the Middle English for "to cut or score the surface of" or as a derivative of the word "scorch." Nonetheless, Scotch whisky pairs beautifully with the caramel flavors of brown sugar and milk and adds a sophisticated, grown-up character.

Ingredients

2 cups milk

1 cup cream

1 tablespoon butter

1 cup brown sugar, unpacked

1/2 teaspoon kosher salt

1/4 cup cornstarch

4 egg yolks

1/4 teaspoon vanilla extract

1 tablespoon Scotch whisky (optional)

8 pint-size, ovenproof glass jars with lids

Directions

In a medium bowl, combine milk and cream. Measure about 1/2 cup of the milk-cream mixture and reserve in a separate bowl. Melt butter and brown sugar with salt in a medium saucepan and cook over medium heat for 2-3 minutes.

Pouring slowly and carefully, add the larger portion of the milk-cream mixture to the pan, whisking constantly until sugar dissolves. While the cream-sugar mixture in the pan is heating, combine reserved 1/2 cup milk-cream mixture with the cornstarch in a small bowl, and whisk to make a slurry with no remaining clumps of cornstarch.

Boil cream-sugar mixture for 2-3 minutes. It will get foamy, so be careful the pan doesn't overflow. Remove from heat and slowly add cornstarch slurry to the cream-sugar mixture while whisking. Return pan to heat, and boil for about 1 minute, stirring constantly until thick. Remove from heat.

In a small bowl, beat egg yolks. Slowly add about 1/4 cup of the hot pudding mixture to beaten egg yolks, whisking constantly to temper the yolks. Then add yolks to pan and whisk thoroughly. (The residual heat will cook the yolks.) Add vanilla and Scotch whisky, if using.

Pour into individual glass jars or let cool for a few minutes and pour into disposable cups. Allow the pudding to set in the refrigerator for at least 3 hours. On chilly evenings, Butterscotch Pudding can also be enjoyed slightly warm.

 Note: If pint-size glass jars are not available, you can use large plastic cups.

Drinks

tips to make serving easy

Make all cold drinks in large sealable pitchers, and transport
in coolers filled with ice.

Serve drinks in double-walled paper cups to help keep drinks cold or hot and to
prevent plastic cups from accidentally being blown overboard.

Safety is always number one on the water. Please drink responsibly.
For recipes that include alcohol, you may want to set aside
a serving for the skipper to enjoy after the boat is safely ashore.

Each recipe in this section serves 6-8.

White Sangria (gf, v, df) Makes about 2 quarts

Startlingly, "sangria" is the Spanish word for bloodletting. This describes the deep red color of sangria as it is most commonly made: with red wine. This white sangria variation is a bit lighter and more refreshing. For an even lighter version, substitute sparkling water for the sparkling wine to make a delicious spritzer.

Ingredients

1/2 Bosc pear, peeled and sliced

1/2 Granny Smith apple, peeled and sliced

1/2 cantaloupe or honeydew melon, cut into 1-inch cubes

1 peach, chopped

2 plums, chopped

1 bottle white wine (Pinot Grigio or Sauvignon Blanc)

1 bottle Prosecco or sparkling white wine

For a creative touch: Experiment with different fruit combinations.

Directions

Combine fruit and still wine in a large pitcher. Allow to rest in the refrigerator for several hours before serving or overnight. Just before serving, combine with equal parts sparkling wine or, if desired, sparkling water.

Phyllis' Frozen Margaritas (gf, v, df) Makes about 1 1/2 quarts

This recipe is named for Jon's Aunt Phyllis, who makes the best frozen margaritas. Frozen limeade makes a better, cleaner-tasting margarita than any commercial margarita mixes we have tried.

Ingredients

1 (12-ounce) can frozen limeade concentrate

6 ounces tequila (silver or reposado)

3 ounces orange liqueur, such as Triple Sec or Cointreau

Ice, crushed or cubed

Note: Silver tequila will have a stronger "bite", whereas reposado tequila will be somewhat smoother in flavor.

Directions

Combine limeade concentrate with tequila and orange liqueur, using the limeade can to measure. Use the limeade can to measure 3 cans of ice cubes (about 36 ounces or 4 loose cups). Combine all ingredients into a blender; blend, working in batches, if necessary. More ice can be added for a thicker texture, if desired. Serve immediately.

Note: This can also be made ahead and kept in the freezer. If frozen, let soften at room temperature for about 20 minutes before serving.

Rhubarb Cooler with Ginger Ale (gf, v, df) Makes about 3 quarts

A unique and refreshing nonalcoholic cooler, this drink is great for kids and adults of all ages.

Ingredients

4 cups water

4 cups rhubarb, coarsely sliced (about 2 stalks)

1/2 cup sugar

2/3 cup fresh squeezed orange juice (about 2 oranges)

2 liters ginger ale, chilled

Directions

In a medium saucepan, combine water, rhubarb and sugar. Bring to a boil, reduce heat and simmer until rhubarb is soft, approximately 15 minutes, stirring occasionally. Let rhubarb mixture cool slightly; strain liquid into a large pitcher using a colander. Add orange juice and ginger ale to pitcher, and mix well. Place pitcher in the refrigerator for 2 to 4 hours to cool before serving. Alternatively, combine all ingredients except the ginger ale. Chill rhubarb mixture in the refrigerator overnight. Add chilled ginger ale immediately before serving.

Waikiki "Mai Tai" (gf, v, df) Makes about 1 1/2 quarts

Inspired by the Mai Tais at the Barefoot Bar on Waikiki Beach, this is not the typical Mai Tai recipe. Always use fresh pineapple when possible. Blackstrap rum adds a touch of sweet molasses flavor that perfectly complements fresh pineapple.

Ingredients

2 cups fresh pineapple, chilled and cut into chunks

2 cups ice cubes

1/2 cup white rum

1/4 cup blackstrap rum

Water as needed

For a creative touch: Add 1 cup coconut milk before blending for a tropical piña colada.

Directions

Combine pineapple, ice and rums in a blender; blend until smooth. Add water to reach desired consistency. Serve immediately, or make ahead and store in the freezer. To serve from frozen, remove from freezer and let soften at room temperature for about 20 minutes before serving.

Sparkling Lemonade (gf, v, df) Makes a little over 2 quarts

This is our version of the classic summer cooler. Try mixing equal amounts with Southern Sweet Tea (page 77) to make an Arnold Palmer.

Ingredients

2/3 cup simple syrup

Juice from 6 lemons

64 ounces club soda, chilled

Directions

To make simple syrup, dissolve 2/3 cup sugar with 1 cup water in a small saucepan over medium heat. Bring to a boil; remove from heat, and cool to room temperature. Simple syrup can be stored in the refrigerator for up to a few weeks in advance. Combine all ingredients in a large pitcher, and mix well. Serve over ice.

Bloody Marys (gf, v, df) Makes about 2 quarts

These can be made without alcohol, if desired. Try them alongside Bloody Mary skewers (page 9).

Ingredients

64 ounces Spicy Hot V8 juice, chilled

Juice from 1 orange

1 tablespoon celery salt

1/4 teaspoon Worcestershire

1 cup vodka

Directions

Combine all ingredients in a large pitcher, and mix well. Serve over ice.

Southern Sweet Tea (gf, v, df) Makes a generous half-gallon

Our version is cold brewed and flavored with fresh orange and lemon.

Ingredients

1/2 gallon warm water

1/2 cup sugar

4 bags black tea

1/2 lemon, seeds removed and sliced

1/2 orange, quartered

Directions

Combine water and sugar in a large pitcher and stir to combine until sugar is dissolved. Add remaining ingredients into the pitcher, and mix well. Place pitcher in the refrigerator overnight to cool.

Spiced Apple Cider Makes a generous gallon

Warm apple cider and sweet spice are great for a brisk day on the water.

Ingredients

1 gallon apple cider

1 tablespoon whole cloves

1 tablespoon whole allspice

1 cinnamon stick

1 cup rum (optional)

Directions

Pour apple cider into a large saucepan. Place cloves and allspice inside a tea ball. Add tea ball and cinnamon stick to cider. Heat cider over medium heat until just simmering. Reduce heat to low; steep cider with spices for 20 minutes. Remove cinnamon stick and tea ball. Add rum, if desired, and stir to combine. Place cider in a large thermos or heatproof pitcher. Serve warm.

Index

About the Authors

Erin grew up in Minnesota; with its 10,000 lakes, water was never far away. One of her favorite places is the family cabin, where pontoon rides and guests were always part of the scene. Jon grew up on the Carolina coast, where he loved the water and all the varying cuisines that his state had to offer. Both Erin and Jon are huge food enthusiasts with a passion for outdoor activity, travel, learning about different cuisines and trying new foods. As adventurous home cooks, they apply the same appreciation and discovery of good food to their own cooking.